ALL IN A RAINFOREST DAY

By ELLEN B. SENISI

Photographs by THOMAS MARENT

Morning sunshine wakes up the rainforest.
Beams of light touch the tops of the tree canopy.

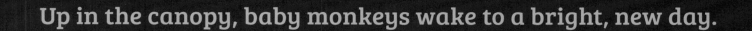

Up in the canopy, baby monkeys wake to a bright, new day.

The sun's rays stream through the forest.
Trees and plants soak in the light they need to grow.

The understory is tangled with vines and branches.
A katydid crawls along in the morning light.

Light filters down to flowers growing on the forest floor.

Daylight shines on waterfalls, streams, and pools of water.

Time for breakfast!

Rainforest creatures look around for food. But they have to look out for themselves, too—so they don't get eaten!

Watch out! Gulp!

Rainforest creatures have developed many different ways to keep from being eaten. Bugs can find safety in numbers as they march along together.

Bugs with prickly bodies can also stay safe. If an animal tries to eat this caterpillar, it will get a mouth full of stinging needles!

Any animal who tries to make a meal of these stink bugs will be sprayed with a stinking, stinging poison that goes deep into its eyes and skin.

Hiding is also a good defense. A gecko blends into leaves on the forest floor. Can you find it?

This poison dart frog doesn't have to hide. Its bright color lets other animals know that they will be poisoned if they eat it!

At noon, the sun is high in the sky. It is dry, hot, and windy in the emergent layer at the top of the forest.

The day looks different on the forest floor. Just a little light finds its way through the thick layer of leaves above.

Suddenly, the weather changes.
Raindrops splash and splatter in the forest.

Rain filters through the trees.
The plants drink up the drops.

Rainforest plants need water
to stay thick and green.

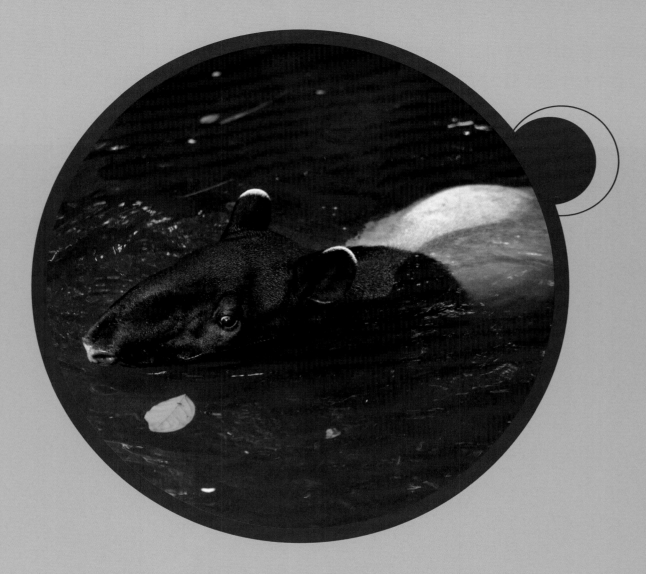

Rainforest animals also need water to live.

Rotting plants and dead creatures crumble into the dark dirt of the forest floor. This makes the soil rich with plant food.

Every day, new plants push their way out of the soil and into the light.

This day is almost over. Animals look for places to sleep as daylight fades.

Darkness comes early on the rainforest floor.

Up high in the canopy, birds watch the last light of day.

Mothers say goodnight
to their babies.

The sun goes down and the forest gets dark.

Animals that have slept all day
wake up and look for food.

Night sounds ring through the forest but the baby animals sleep.

A silver moon rises over the trees. Another rainforest day is over.

Rainforests have 4 different layers. From top to bottom they are:

Emergent layer: at the very top of the rainforest; lots of sun up here.

Canopy: a layer of tree branches below the emergent layer; it's fairly sunny and many animals live here.

Understory: between the canopy and the ground; not much sunlight gets through here.

Forest floor: at the bottom of the rainforest; it's shady down here.

Text copyright 2014 © Ellen B. Senisi

Photographs copyright 2014 © Thomas Marent except cover photo and page 22: 2014 © Ellen B. Senisi

Edited by Monica Maxwell-Paegle

Designed by Kate Greene at Owl's Head Solutions, Inc.

EdTechLens Publishing

www.edtechlens.com

Summary: Factual text and authentic photographs show plants and animals of the rainforest throughout a day from morning to night.

Library of Congress Control Number: 2013956188